Praise for *Those We Can No Longer See*

Bob Ross is a master of lyric delicacy red-threaded through dramas of rural humor, darkness, and loss. His music often surprises a reader, as it does in the prologue. The stanzas move forward with mysterious jauntiness, inviting us to dance right through to where *The stove is ticking and the room is cold/ and the moon is down and the stars are old/ and the house where I earned my confidence/ is nowhere.* This authentic voice of the Nebraska landscape is fine cause for celebration.

Sandra Alcosser, author of *A Fish to Feed All Hunger* and *Except by Nature*

Bob Ross's *Those We Can No Longer See* is a book of ghosts, some eulogized, some quietly cursed. Storm clouds furl in "the sky's taken on an anvil's elegance;" a mother is hauntingly remembered as "Nothing left of her now/ but an anxious voice in my dreams"; and a rural home is evoked with "It was the horizon I fell in love with/ a circle of hills that held me/ closer than I knew." People, dogs, times and places are brought temporarily back to life in Ross's crisp, imaginative language.

Matt Mason, Nebraska State Poet and author of *I Have a Poem the Size of the Moon*

Those We Can
No Longer See

New and Selected Poems

BOB ROSS

This book of poems is dedicated to Harry Duncan and Donald Moccasin,
men of learning, of gentle voices and generous hearts.

Acknowledgments

Several of these poems have been published elsewhere under different titles; some appeared as reprinted here, while others are much revised. Thanks go to all editors of literary magazines and anthologies, who labor to shelter a minstrel traffic from the storm of events.

The first part of "1939 (male, female)" was in *Solitary Confinement*, published by Abattoir Editions, Omaha, Nebraska, 1975.

"Dream Lyric" (under the title "Night Lyric") appeared in *As Far as I Can See*, edited by Charles Woodward, 1989.

Part of "Barn Wood" was in *Solitary Confinement* under the title "Learning: Boards."

"Wren Sonata," parts thereof, appeared in *CutBank* under the title "Letter to a Dead Wren." Later, it was in the *Heartland* feature of *The Fairbanks Daily News-Miner*. The full version most like the present one appeared in *Puerto del Sol*.

"The Loss" was in *The Sandhills and Other Geographies: An Anthology of Nebraska Poetry*, edited by Mark Sanders.

Two opening stanzas of "Voices," under the title "Dusk," and a full version of "Light" were in a chapbook published in 1991 by Twin Pines Press, also titled *Light*.

"Grouse" was in *The Decade Dance*, edited by Mark Sanders. It was also printed as part of a chapbook by Catherine Miller under the title "Just Out of Range."

"Angina" first appeared in *Prairie Schooner*.

"The Junk Man's Truck," "Kitchen," "News," and "After the Dinner Party" were in *basalt*.

"Stove Wood" appeared in *Nebraska Humanities* under the title "Moving Day: Goodbye to the Big Elm."

Part of "Winter Count," under the title "Tree," was published in *Nebraska Presence, An Anthology of Poetry*, edited by Greg Kosmicki and Mary K. Stillwell.

"Who Cares" first appeared in *Heartland*.

"Land" appeared in *Prairie Schooner* and was republished in *As Far as I Can See*.

"The Torpedo Angel" was published in *Heartland* and *Kansas Quarterly*, then reprinted in *A Garland for Harry Duncan*, an anthology edited by W. Thomas Taylor.

Contents

I work in the night, surrounded by stars,
by trees, by crickets, by molecules of despair
at my desk in the middle of the air.

No sirens, no ambulances, barely a road,
no newspaper, no Taco Cabana.
There's a town if I wanted to go there.

There's no one awake within a mile.
There's a dog on the bed with a dream in his head
and another little dog in a chair.

The stove is ticking and the room is cold
and the moon is down and the stars are old
and the house where I earned my confidence
is nowhere.

1939 (male, female)

Eloquent as knives, barn swallows
part and splice the loaded air. Rain crows cry and spiral,
dive-bomb the updrafts.
What moves on land is eyes northwest, astonished:
the sky's taken on an anvil's elegance.
Something iron is coming. It looks miles high.

"Some wind in that."
But the cottonwoods are barely whispering,
the windmill's stopped.

No school you've been to but what you can remember
to help you read this, no trying to stare it down.
It's gray as the *World-Herald*'s futures column,
top and edges white as dimes,
but the sun no more shines through it
than the egg money through last month's bank statement.
Black tinted green means hail
suspended in a fist of wind.

Your hatband's
oily on your forehead; sweat
sticks like honey in the groove of your back,
the backs of your hands sweat.
The work has to get done sometime, you keep at it
while you can, you know how long it takes
to get to the house, you won't be caught in it
this time. Another row, up and down,
time to quit.
You drive in

among the excited yard animals and collected
woods and metals of your life
to someone, a stranger half yourself
whom you may call "your" woman,
and the summer's dust begins to rise and swirl and shift—

The two of you stand there,
armed with each other, facing
all the roll-call thunders of the world,
rooted in tame grass fenced in, what you hope is happiness,
watching it come on, praying no fire, not too much wind,
no hail to murder your crops
but rain, rain; and what can be done
is done. The first drop spats your shirt,
more clack on the tin roof. You go in
to coffee. WNAX would be crashing like blitzkreig.
Nothing much to do in a storm's time

but put your hands together, listen,
stare at the kitchen window, and hold on.

That was the year before his father died.
That was the year before I lost the baby.
The year before we gave up on the farm.
The year before we all stopped smiling.

That was the year of the phony war in Europe.
That was the year we could have made some money.
That was the year before we both went quiet.
That was the year before I moved to Wood Lake.

That year I turned twenty-eight in the fall.
The county could see I was loved. My breasts stood high.
That year I began to see ahead.
That year I felt confident.

I named her Mary Alice. She was dead.
When they told me that they said to me You'll get over it.
Over it! Oh, my God! Get over it!
After that year I never looked young again.

Dream Lyric

Eerie, eerie, wind in crooked limbs.
A hoot-owl mocks the mice. Wind-packed snow
grunts like tired horses.
I stalk the grove in awkward, tearing cold.

Weed-stems tick and buzz.
A few have crowns. The seed I jolt
skids like dust under the trees,
a line of twisted 80-year-old willows.

Starlight and snowlight frame a stucco house.
Smoke jitters downwind from the chimney.
One kerosene-lit window. Midnight yowls and roars.

She puts away her sewing, whuffs the lamp.
December 1943.
This frost breaks iron. I have no business here.

Barn Wood

1.

There was this ranch,
in Nebraska, in the ranching country.
There were buildings,
a house, barn, sheds, corrals, a shop,
a wellhouse—
There were always a few boards lying around.
If you wanted to fix something you got a board;
if you wanted to block a hole,
prop up something to the right height,
you found a board.

Maybe you'd find it out in the chicken coop
    or behind the loading chute;
maybe it'd be deep in grass and hard to see
and when you picked it up there'd be crickets or beetles
    or an ant colony, or angleworms or grubworms,
    or a snake.
If it'd been there very long it'd be two-sided,
    smooth and board-colored on the bottom side
    and rough and gray or silver on the top.

Maybe there'd be nails in it.
Maybe it'd be rotten or warped or split
but you could saw off the bad end and use the rest,
    lots of times you wouldn't need a good one,
    just something to fool the cattle;
or a board might look rotten but be sound wood inside,
    if you hit it on the ground you could tell
    by the feel.

Sometimes a board would get so lost
you'd find it by accident.
You'd be digging a post-hole and the diggers would hit
and there it'd be,
sand sticking to it, roots growing through
cracks and nail holes,
lying in a smell of dirt
asleep on a mirror of quiet rot.

Pull it up and give it a toss.
The hell with it.

2.

Somewhere an ambulance starts its motor.
A door in the air has closed.
Oh, the money, the money,
sell the place and take the money,
sooner or later, sooner better than later.
Who's to prevent you? Didn't you always need it?
Let the grove go to ruin, let spurge take the meadow,
leave the windmill towers to fall down by themselves.

Nothing remains of the pole barn
but a skeleton of posts.
Some scavenger has taken the boards.
They're behind the counter of a Cracker Barrel
like the one where we used to stop to buy mints for Leslie.
All that sunburned ignorance,
porcelain doll's head found in a blowout,
flint arrowheads under sand—
Below them all, the bones of ancient bison.

3.

Most of us quit, and the land takes care of itself,
or it doesn't.
You can drive the road from Long Pine
and not see ten sets of buildings.
You'll pass a ranch turned over to the state
for research and grasslands recreation.
Cows are rotated through pastures
on a schedule to control the weeds.
They control the sunflowers.

Sunrise,
first light touching the meadow—
Those lucky enough to see it
come and go as tourists.
On the drive back to St. Louis,
I-80, I-25, I-70,
they pass a dozen Cracker Barrels
selling samplers stitched in Thailand in country colors:
"God bless our home."

Wren Sonata: The Parts of Speech
(Missoula, 1981)

1. *The event.*

I saw part of it:
Calico's tail jerking,
her leap, and
Pepper bullying the cat.
I robbed her in turn,
found myself holding
cocky you. Too-
Little, I sat
on the tailgate of a used-out truck.
The day, the work
slid from my shoulders.

Your wings, the princely feathers,
inch pinions banded rust-brown,
elm bark color exactly.
Soft gray underneath,
tight fan. The joinery of flight.

Your feet curled tightly,
grasping. You began to be
mauled with my handling.
I gave you back to Callie
for her unborn kittens,
said I was not moved.

(That quiet
hour, the sun
pivoted on you.)

2. *The fear.*

Wren, I've watched
my uncle, a worn-tough farmer,
rest his hip on a post after milking,
facing the marbled and rayed and blazing west,
letting a striped kitten chew his thumb,
the same man capable of coming drunk
to work not done and the light gone
and beating his thin-skinned Guernseys
to a weird confusion:
floor of the milk-barn slick with manure,
spilled grain everywhere, a stall in splinters,
him turning, blind with anger,
no one speaking.

Here is the worst thing I've done.
I had a wild dog once, a stray.
He came to love me
and I him. When I was gone
a few days he left the place.
He didn't return when I came home.

It was winter.
Nights later I was sure he was dead.
A howl came from Hagan Lake.
I heard it once, clearly.
It was dark. I was uneasy in the dark.
I didn't go look for him.

Years later, I learned how he died,
leg caught in a coyote trap,
alone in the middle of a frozen lake.

3. *When have I had courage?*

We sat together in the cab of the pickup
in front of Krejeski's ranch house.
The stars shook and the snow crawled
in little twists across the yard.
It was cold.

Listen, I said, you can get a job in town.
She said, Are you looking for a free ride.
We sat there,
eyes wet with the tenderness we'd been making,
windows frosted over,
no one speaking.
That was the dead time
when summer's kittens lay frozen under the wellhouse,
when cattle wept because of the wind
and the tears clung hard and dirty on their cheeks for days.

It's past two o'clock, she said.
I have to go inside.

4. *A cry must come from me.*

When I was not so sober, and tighter in my skin,
the drunk man's neighbor, pain was what I believed in.
A bull on a clothesline needled me then.

>   Wren! You are great Nature's word
>   for lightness and exactitude
>   shrug of the sun
>   wink of cloud
>   comma of air and verb of blood

>   Lingo of purpose
>   spiel of wants

sweet hope's logic and passion's fret
persuasive as an infant's hands
piercing as cirrus high at night

Brag me the giant speech of spring
the summer jabber that packs your veins
No leaf will thrust
no planet spin
lacking the rhetoric of wrens.

(Dear to me without my knowing,
killed so neatly I could not find the wound.)

5. *In the room with the patched pillow.*

Kitty kitty? The cat has my tongue.
Words are holes in my mouth.
Can I speak without shrieking?
I've a death I must celebrate,
a wish, a love light and long cherished.

A woman fine as moss roses,
sweet as butter and warm as milk,
has crossed my purposes with a no.
Her heart's hied off in no direction,
just damned elsewhere.
It hurt so bad, I couldn't feel a thing.

Let go, let go, sharp notes tell me.
I hold her little waist in my palm's eye
until flesh is stripped from my hands
like the time we roped that big three-year-old
colt for castrating.
The smallest measure of magic
is to put back life in a dead wren.
If I had the smallest magic I'd have made her love me.

Aiee! Falling!
I'm a lost pendulum,
a blade, a white distance,

I fall forward, clutching my belly,
to bite the belly of the fabric.
The scream comes of itself.

6. *Prayer.*

Language, blessing and terror of man,
your death will do for all of us.
When the apple fell
and longing reddened the stubborn lips of Eve,
your song burst forth in Heaven.
We have our legacy.
No passion without hurt,
no love without the odor of entrails.

Ascend,
carry a message, Cat-kissed:

pray for all us love's-leftovers
that we continue (on our wires,

each his own) to be torn
by songs these tender mornings

and that we may
find occasionally
listeners
according to our likings,

Amen.

(I will be tender and angry.
I will touch this grief. I will break my silence for love.)

The Loss

We hunted her in the near west pasture;
fifteen and not sixteen had come in
to water at the tank. I took Steve
and the pickup, intending to bring her
if she could be found, or look for a downed
wire. She was in a low place
not too far from the house.

This in early June, after a weekend
in which one bull got with the cows
and another fought with the neighbor's bull
and tore out twenty rods of fence.
One of them dug a bull-hole
two feet deep and four across,
just right to catch the front end of my truck.
Spring having dragged along with the usual delays,
trips to Lincoln, work not getting done,
my own affairs not going right, another
year gone, I was in no mood
to fool with the damned bulls.
Then this thing happens. On a blue day,
the grass fresh between rains,
a friend along to witness my helplessness,
this little heifer was lying there trying to calve
and couldn't. The dead front legs
stuck out of her sideways and upside down,
the head turned back under the pelvic bone.

Here is the procedure. You go in with a knife,
remove the front legs at the shoulder,
push the calf back in and force the head
straight until you can put the cable on.
Then you battle with the calf-puller,

hoping it doesn't stick again at the hips.
She'd been there for hours. The fluid was gone,
the calf wedged tight, and the flies had found her.
She couldn't stand, no way to load her
to take her to the vet.
I shot her. She seemed
to be expecting it. We dragged the carcass
behind the pickup to a blowout's edge
and rolled it in.

Voices

Night has slipped like a doe
from the brush at the edge of the field.
First darkness wets our feet like the shy
beginnings of mold.

Now the evening star
is a diamond above the low hills,
the air so still—
Listen! There. Two voices.
The old and the dead are whispering.

> *When Doc Lear sewed me after our second baby,*
> *he thought he'd give you back a younger woman.*
> *I was too tight for you then.*
> *I moved into the guest room,*
> *kept my bed there twenty years.*

> > *You never liked it, never wanted me.*
> > *Only as a way of showing love.*

> *That's just wrong.*
> *I'd have been passionate, except—*

> > *You were passionate.*
> > *Most of it was anger.*

> *There was a woman you went to.*
> *You had a woman before me,*
> *you have one now.*
> *There's no need to lie to me.*

We talk, play cards.
What I have is memories.

You have our son. He drives from Lincoln
once a month. He never visits me.

The boy is not much company.
He yawns, stretches, flips the TV,
never stays long, glad to get away.
We do not talk of essential things.

Then he's like you.

Like you,
a nitpicker, carrier of grudges.
Has no more sense with money than a cat.

He has sense enough.
What a smart boy he was!
I took such pride in him, the way he passed his tests,
the way he showed that bragging sister of mine.
Smarter than all his cousins put together.

So smart he couldn't tell one cow from another.
You turned his head with your talk about his test scores
till he thought he'd never work a day in his life.
I wanted a son for the business.
He won't take risks. He can't finish things.

I wanted him to use that brain of his,
not to worry about cattle and money.
You thought and worried plenty. Where's your money?
It was a cheap coffin you buried me in.

It cost more than that car you bought just before I met you.

And your old car! If I had to ride in that!
The door flew open and the seat slid out.
I had to hold you tight going round the corners.

You weren't ashamed to marry a poor man.

Ashamed of you! The kindest man I knew.
In your way you were handsome,
Humphrey Bogart in plow shoes.
When we danced, I thought you were Fred Astaire.
I couldn't keep up with you.

> *I fell when I first saw you,*
> *fell literally, tripped and landed*
> *on my chin, right there in the post office.*
> *If I'd known then what I know now—*

If I'd known then what I know now—

> *I'd do it over. Didn't we have a life?*
> *Didn't we make the hens cackle?*

Didn't we have plenty to cry about?
Didn't we laugh?

> *Yet you didn't want me.*

Never say so. You don't know a woman's heart.
I want you now, I want you here
beside me in the earth— I mean, the gravel.
Look at yourself! Back curled like a snail,
eighty-four years old. Eighty-four hard years!
What are you waiting for?

> *You know I'm inclined to trip if I rush my steps.*
> *I'll come when I can.*

White

Snow and quiet, quiet and snow.
This is the night of vertigo.

A frozen couple lie in bed.
Their cat blinks, she lowers her head.

The stars burn their acetylene,
the rat rages in the barn.

Wash of moonlight, white as bone.
A child was born who did not come home.

Without comfort, without rest,
night of sorrow unexpressed,

bitter memory, over-and-done.
Impacted passion clots the mind.

What rider pauses on the road,
bony horse and drawn hood?

Little wild dogs up on the hill,
keep still, lie still.

The Grass Widow: Homesteading in Western Nebraska

1. The Boys

If there were going to be houses
we wanted them unpainted
If there were going to be fences
we wanted them tight and straight
(how the naked sunlight shone
on the gleaming double wire
that marked the absent rancher's bogus claim)

We roamed and played forever
in that Edenic land
till our overalls fell in tatters
till we turned bronze like lizards
while the tall wind sucked our parents
clean of everything.

2. Him

Days of furnace wind
had turned our corn to paper
and blown a sickness in the old cow's gluey eyes
I had given the horse his oats
and was sitting on him bareback
my ankle across his neck
digging at a cactus thorn in my heel

A horse is not a sofa
Maybe a bee

I found myself in air
upside down
then the ground broke my leg

Seeing her at the cultivator
under that awful sun
all I could think of
all in God's bountiful world I could think of
was California.

3. Her

After he left us
the boys flew wild as geese
More and more I found myself alone

It was not so bad
being alone
A man who stopped by sometimes
must have told his friends
More and more I was visited

A girl was planted in me
hair golden like the tassels
of corn we never grew
When I saw her at my breast
I knew I would make a life here

The barren furrows are gone
the scars we caused have healed
the sand has forgotten us

I died in a little town
where a hundred sorry windmills

clanked and squealed above a hundred houses
I carried myself proud
Whatever the old men said of me
I knew they'd once sobbed their bitterness
and longed to go home

Here was my home
I gave the land
one useless drunk one teacher
and one cattleman
It was the horizon I fell in love with—
a circle of hills that held me
closer than I knew.

Good Luck, Long Life, A Thousand Wishes

A front comes in from Canada and they come, too,
above the leaves, below the contrails. Calling.
They ride so high, sometimes you think you imagine them.
There. You point, but it's an eyespot

until, if you're lucky, their wings flare against the sun.
Say "Ah." Your mouth is open.
A crane may live as long as a man.
Some cranes. Some men. Long life not guaranteed.

To lie looking up at cranes
as a boy looks up at leaves,
thinking the breeze might talk to him,
I want to be laid face to the sky,
if I must truly leave this pretty world
so small and sweet and green and dear to me.

Light

Branches ice-broken from Chinese elms
lie ungathered on the yellow lawns.
A white-haired woman chases blowing paper
searching for a letter from her long-dead son.
In merciless light at the end of winter,
I'm home in the town at the end of the road.

> *Pintails and mallards rest from the windroad,*
> *blackbirds in thousands flood the bare elms.*
> *A delighted old dog tours the neighbors' lawns*
> *and woofs at the kid who brings the paper.*
> *At coffee, they josh my father's son*
> *and tally the ones who didn't winter.*

The bowl of the sky is cracked by winter
and gray dust sifts across the road.
Each house has its pair of shoddy elms
to buckle the sidewalk and rob the lawn.
No news ever is allowed in the paper
but "Farmer's daughter marries rancher's son."

> *Everyone's loved and wayward son,*
> *I come with the dust that follows winter*
> *to scrape my father for cash for the road*
> *and haul the branches from the ice-trimmed elms.*
> *I'm a blackbird honored on every lawn,*
> *the proudest counterfeit on paper.*

The wall of my chest is wasps'-nest paper,
two wrinkled onions my only sons.

My bootsoles scuffle the drag of winter
as I hunch and shoulder the sleety road
past childhood grudges under swollen elms
where dandelions sprawl in the unraked lawns.

These streets have houses, the houses have lawns
and on every doorstep there's a Sunday paper.
Dads read comics to their wriggling sons
while the morning sun climbs the back of winter
and steams the frost from the empty road.
Some calming magic has webbed these elms. . . .

One bare-lawn elm grows through the paper
to spill hooked shadows on the winter road,
to thrust a root and trip a small-town son.

Grouse

The birds get up. Too far, they're out of range.
My father stands, a hunchback with a gun,
and lets them fly off cackling into morning.

No shot. No grouse, but good enough for lies
to prod a brother, white in Arizona.
The birds fly up. Too far. They're out of range.

Dave and Duke. Those bankers. Kenny Graff.
Along the lake, impatient in the blinds—
The bankers fly off cackling into morning

and Pop ejects the shells. I pick him up
and drive down one more ridge, back toward the house.
The birds are smart. They get up out of range.

He's 81. Each fall I think the same:
this hunt will be our last. Today is gold,
the minutes rise up cackling. In the morning

I leave for Provincetown. My father loves me,
he's chilled, he's tired, he wants a cigarette
to stun his heart to silence. Out of range

a hawk is circling, showing us the grouse.
They're everywhere. We shoot them every year.
Their lift-off cackle's loud as guns this morning.
The fat birds fly away, just out of range.

Billings

Last night on the way to Billings
I crimped a fender of my father's brand-new truck.
We were on I-90, me driving.
While I bent to look at the damage,
he went off to get more coffee.
Then I couldn't find him.

I sold that International pile
of rust and caked-on cowshit
to Alan Yates in the summer of '84.
I had just replaced the engine.
That happened to be the year my mother died,
same year I moved to Alaska.

In a decade I re-invent nightly,
my parents appear as old photographs
edged with sweat-smudges and thumb-stains.
I open my mouth to yell at them.
"Explain yourselves, damn you old people."
Never an answer.

Past seventy and nobody,
in dreams I'm a young man driving across the plains.
No plans. No connections. Going to Montana.
In my dead father's dream, he steps off a bus
in Hayfork, California,
where uncles he hasn't seen in ninety years
greet him, their cracked teeth full of gold.

Cataracts

1.

I wonder what my father thought about.
He would fall asleep in front of the TV,
shuffle to bed (his snores would shake the house),
then wake up early, 2 or 3 a.m.,
play solitaire, smoke, drink coffee,
go for breakfast when the café opened,
6 a.m.

I do not think he thought about selling real estate.

My mom and I'd wake up and dress for school.
He'd be back home by then, all ours,
husband, father, turner of the world's wheel
and known. But what did he think about
at that hard Formica table,
cigarette smoke ribboning upward
in the dark?

2.

Even if stolen from the depth of night
when no one else can use it,
each moment taken
to watch a snowflake fall or write a poem
is bread grabbed from the mouths of the abundant poor.
Love ripped from the hearts of those who depend on us.
Is bitter death postponed at the expense of strangers.
I don't know if my father felt regret,
or if he thought he was getting away with something.

3.

The footsteps of those we can no longer see
surround us. 2 a.m.
The air in this room looks smoky, but
it's only these damned cataracts.

Sand Cherries

I didn't know I loved sand cherries
until the day my father stopped the car
and went down into the road ditch
with his hat in his hand

gravel road
1972 Ford car
work hat
short-brimmed Stetson

together we picked a hatful
in less than half an hour
Fifteen miles to Long Pine
I balanced them on my knee
like a dark-eyed baby

Aunt Myra baked the cherries into a pie
they didn't make a big pie
Each of us ate one slice
with vanilla ice cream

My mother does not show up in this picture
Hot sun, late June
dry-mouth tang of summer
smell of alkali leaves

Ed and Alice, Oz and Myra
those people I knew and did not know
how much I loved

Angina

Mother brought a guest into the house
and kept him. Twenty years at the table,
Dad with his bloodhound courage, me with my possum eye,
silent in his presence. We called him Pain.

Could not get in a word while he was speaking.
If one of us would touch her,
a quick glance toward his feet. Permission, modesty.
Said she loved us. Poured his coffee first.

This maggot built his castle in her heart
till every blush was his, each careful movement.
Over stale Rice Chex we coughed and changed our plans
while she lolled in bed with that bastard son of a prince.

None of us guessed she had a second lover
until the day *his* soft glove shattered the door.
She put down her fork, stood up, and left Pain with us.
He threw a tantrum while we swept up rusty screws.

The creep's still here. Last night in the kitchen
his hand was on Pop's arm. I had to say something.
"Listen, you two depress me, this is weird,
I won't put up with it. The sponger goes, or me."

The look they gave each other set me reeling.
My father's voice was sad and far away.
"Son, looks like we've finished off the braunschweiger.
I have to go to bed. Entertain our friend."

There we were. Pain opened the fridge,
got the Old Crow out and poured me a third of a glass.
"What do you want?" I whispered. "I'll give anything,
only leave this house at once!" The wan thing smiled.

"Bob," he said, "you know I admire you,
but it's getting late and you've got a long drive ahead.
Unfold the map. I know every shard in the road,
let me help you plan your trip. Sit down," he said.

The Junk Man's Truck

The junk man's truck was so old
it ran by steam.
He would turn the boiler off
at the foot of the hill
and it would go on pressure
up and up
slowly and more slowly
to the top where the junk man lived.

This was my mother's memory,
not mine.
Nothing ran by steam
past the middle of the 1950s,
not even railroad engines
any more.

The last time I saw her,
she begged me to forget writing
and get my teaching certificate.
Thirty years ago.

Nothing left of her now
but an anxious voice in my dreams,
cold stone in a sandy graveyard,
and the junk man's truck
hissing slowly and more slowly
up the hill.

Kitchen

This is to let you know I've rebuilt the kitchen.
I hired Frank Williams to add a triple window
and raise the air conditioner where you sat and smoked.
I can look out from your table and see robins,
or a cardinal if there is one. Or the garbage men;
the truck comes Wednesday mornings, like it did.

The news is poor. Your friend Floyd Gould is dead,
the neighbor's hard-luck daughter killed herself.
The backyard grass is pushing up its fuzz,
those tulips by the step are coming on.
All winter it's been warm and wet. Our renter
made me an offer to try to buy the ranch.

If only you could see this kitchen window!
And new linoleum, actually vinyl tile,
good stuff, they say. The no-wax kind.
There'll be new cabinets once I get the money.
Your spendthrift son is tight. I watch for deals.
I'll buy some factory seconds and paint to match.

You used to sit here. Both of you'd be smoking.
Two coffee cups, one ash tray, half a loaf of bread,
the window-sash blocked by the air conditioner
so you'd have to stand if you wanted to see outside
or shut it off if you wanted to hear each other—
the plaster slowly cracking above your skulls.

Stove Wood

White woodflakes drift. High up, a chainsaw drones.
One limb cracks free and clubs a dent in the sod.
Jim Grubb has *Love* and *Hate* inked on his fists.
He's come with a helper to take the big tree down.

It's a nuisance elm. The first ice storm
will dump the summer's new growth on the lawn.
Jim's rope-man, Johnny, is making wood for the tenants,
a couple just starting out, twenty and dumb.

"Before I put all this weight on I sure could climb,"
Jim Grubb hollers, a man with the neck of a hog.
"I can still get around in the branches, though, can't I, Johnny?"
"That's right." Johnny winks. "I believe he can get around."
In ten years, when I no longer own it, this house will burn.
Another limb hits the ground.

Suggestions on Leaving the House

Pull the front door closed or leave it open.
Let the shades flap up or pull them down.
Cut the grass or forget it. The grass is
not your problem.

Compton's Encyclopedia stays behind,
its Cyclops, schematic of a Lewis gun.
The calendar stays on the wall. Those glowing girls
are last year's women.

Your bedroom with its cracked ceiling
where starry glints reflected off the plaster.
The bacon smell that never left the kitchen.
Coffee, toast, fresh ink when you opened the paper,
manure from the garden, horseweeds' musky tang.
The sunrise. How it brought forth birdsong. Again and again.

Responsibility
(for Dobbie, who befriended me)

I have been present for the deaths
of more than one
kind animal,

but his hoarse abandoned howl
dying on the black-ice wind
still ribbons me.

Why hast thou forsaken me

My brother sang on his final birthday
a Lakota death song
and I was not there,

and my dad would rather
have had a word about the truth of things
than a hand of gin,

but if I could change one thing
to make my bent life straight
after my last gulp from the bowl of air,

let the keeper of time
take me back in bleak December
to Hagan Lake.

Let me find my poor lost dog,
let me lift his foot from the trap,
let me kiss him, let me pick him up

and whisper, my love, my joy,
my Runs-In-Circles, my furry prankster,
dear one, what have they done to you,

I will bring you home.

No Call, No Foul, No Points for Patty Mills

LaMarcus cans three free throws
and the Spurs pull within a point.
All the weasels in my blood
dance a war chant
and when the Thunder guard inbounds
he slugs Ginobili
no call
sit down, weasels

The ball gets flubbed and flubbed again
and our guys grab it and throw it around
Patty Mills puts up a shot
Airball
and I'm thirteen and my traitor arms
refuse to fight David McClintock
who is beating the hell out of me
for throwing a ripe tomato at his sister.

My life becomes a one-point loss.
Our Subaru blew a head gasket
and I had to sell it cheap.
My testosterone takes refuge in my toenails.
I have four cavities (my wife's shy dentist
is disappointed) and, by the way,
my good friend David McClintock
is dead.

How would it feel (if this is how *this* feels)
to be a mother ululating on a hilltop

watching her strong son topple
in the fight below?
How would it feel to be the pilot
who dropped twelve breathing and joking
firefighters on the wrong
damned ridge?

I have done a few things right,
I once woke my lover up
before she could crash the car,
but my poor Spurs flubbed the ball
and Patty Mills had half a shot
and missed. Oh Jesus Christ,
I could howl and cry
all bloody night.

Toccata for the Day of the Dead
(Mike Lederer, 1946-2007)

Back in that lost decade,
I happened to be walking across campus.
My cousin came out of the Music Building.
"How you doing, Mike?" I seldom saw him.

"Not good." He looked unhappy.
"I need to write a piece for Dr. Ritchie,
but I can't. I'll take an Incomplete in Composition."
That's Mike, I thought, *always with the Incompletes.*

"Why not sit your ass down and write something?"
His blue eyes looked away. He gave a shrug,
this gentle guy who improvised like Monk
and could play anything for woodwind, Mozart to Mahler.

All he said was, "Nothing comes to me."
Wherever I was going must have seemed important.
I wish now I'd forgot where I was going.
I wish I'd never shoved him on the playground.

Nothing comes to you! Nothing comes to you?
It's colon cancer that comes to you.
Turn around! I'm forty years in the future.
Turn around! I know what comes to you.

Cousin, we'll find a piano.
We'll write a toccata because I like the word toccata.
Better yet, you pick and I'll transcribe
those broken riffs when joy last clutched your heart.

Aunt Marian's Polka

Uncle Lyman drives the car.
Aunt Marian rides in back
to pretend her husband's her chauffeur,
but he won't wear the cap.

Uncle Lyman's tall and pink and hearty.
He dives right in and joins the party.
She tastes her drink and narrows her eyes
and gets ready to tell five or six more lies.

Aunt Marian's teeth are long as pencils.
She loves to handle sharp utensils.
She carries a fork out onto the deck
and stares and stares at Lyman's neck.

Her hair is gray, her skin is yellow,
and once she gets some gin inside her
she grabs the nearest handsome fellow
and polkas with him like a tiger.

But when old LPs have lost their charm
and the liquor's drunk and the party's dead,
Uncle Lyman grips her brittle arm
and guides her snarling off to bed.

To the Toy Animals
(for Jemma Miller at eight months)

Crib-companions
with plush acrylic skins,
we pay our respect
to your origins:

remorseless Tiger,
resolute Bear,
driven out by babies
to the who-knows-where.

Banished away
by babies smiling,
babies not soothed
by lullabying,

babies of presidents
and prime ministers
sliding down
the corporate banisters,

babies burnished
like Tiffany lamps,
babies hurried
through refugee camps,

prostitutes' babies
who'll be sold at age ten,
evangelists' babies
who must be Born Again.

The colonel's daughter
who's never gone dirty,
the corporal's son
who'll never see thirty

need some air
and a place to stand.
Only a sip of water,
just an inch of land—

Move over, Tiger.
Move over, Bear.
We place little Jemma
in your care.

Song for Aśke Wiŋ's Baby

I saw your mother when she was beautiful
Spirit Rider through the Black Hills
acorn equestrian helmet
twelve years old and sassy as a jay

I saw your mother when she was young
fifteen and watching the Sun Dance
sober, not looking for a handout
hoping to still be counted among the good

Little child who lies I don't know where
sleep calm in the deep warm night
May the spirits (I don't believe in them) protect you.
I saw your mother when she was a child
before twenty demons swarmed into the house
on their bright glass wings.

Lost on the Great Plains

He recited a poem,
described Paris and Rome,
he played her Chopin and Scarlatti.
She observed with a sigh,
"You're a talented guy,
but I only like Plains Literati."

He peeled her a mango
and danced her the tango,
he showed her his antique Bugatti.
She said, "No offense,
but you seem a bit dense.
I only like Plains Literati."

So he left San Francisco
and moved to Ceresco,
drank malt liquor till he was blotty.
He lived in a trailer
and wrote a crime thriller
and so joined the Plains Literati.

She threw rocks at his head,
said she wanted him dead,
and married a skier named Scotty.
Now she has five divorces,
trains thoroughbred horses,
and speaks no more of Plains Literati.

Some Things We Gave Flaco

He was starving in the woods alone.
We betrayed him with a piece of chicken.

The first thing that we gave him was a bath.
Three soapings on the step at Mariposa
drowned a geography of fleas,
fleas as fat as match heads,
fleas in crowds incredible on such a thin-haired,
bony rat.
We gave him kibble and a room
"until we can find a home for him."
We gave him his name and a collar
and a bed.
We gave him a trainer, six weeks of sessions
so he'd stop shrieking at the neighbors.
He kept shrieking at the neighbors.

We gave him walks on the leash
and a routine.
We gave him companions.
We gave him a sweater.
We gave him pills and vaccinations.
We gave him, in summer,
a place to run and bark at buzzards
and sniff the urine of rabbits and coyotes.

We gave him bits of chicken
and bits of turkey
and his piece of cheese whenever we opened the cheese

and his corner of the occasional ginger snap.
We taught him to sit and to shake hands
and gave him praise when he was good
and a thousand useless lectures when he wasn't
and a place by the fire when there was a fire
and, when it was hot, a place on the couch
below the air conditioner.

We gave him rides in the car
and rides in the pickup truck.
We gave him wild bedtime tug-of-wars
with his hedgehog, and, once he'd calmed,
we gave him the hedgehog.
He slept with us, and we took him where we could.
We could not take him everywhere.

Because the x-rays told us
our Flaco was dying of cancer
we betrayed him to a gentler death
that he did not understand
because he'd believed we loved him
and because nobody understands.
He went to it alone
though we stood by him at the table
and stroked his head, and his paws,
because to die is always
to become no one
and to go alone.

He gave us warmth, he gave us laughter,
he gave us consternation, he gave us
his furious, enlarged heart, he gave us
all he had.

48

Winter Count

1.

In the year of two comets
we taught at a Lakota college,
an 80-mile drive each way.
We passed a lone cow standing
in the corner of a fence
(same cow, same fence corner)
at the same time every morning.
Slowly we came to realize
she'd been frozen solid there.
That winter must have been cold.

2.

The woman I imagine
is neither thin nor beautiful.
Her hair hangs loose and black
and sways at her hips.
She owl-dances, eyes downcast,
hot and fluid beneath her deerskin dress,
patterned beads and shawl.
No virgin, she has had a man,
more than one, she will have another
tonight.
            Indifferent to them all,
she moves up and down,
mindful of the drum.
Firelight softens her face. Deep shadow behind.
A whole dark continent
full of enemies.

3.

Suppose you are fifteen and beautiful
with a fine pair of black upslanting eyes,
but instead of living in a nice suburban house
and fighting with your mother over homework
and boys and TV and whether you cleaned your room
you live with your father when you can find him
(so busy with his drugs and with his women)
or with a 19-year-old lover
who practices the detached look of a criminal
who follows you like your shadow
and who knows nothing useful—

you might dream a tree
that springs straight up from the ground
with roots that entwine your grandmothers
trunk silver as the moon
two shimmering branches lifted to the sky.
Each leaf would have a thousand shapes
each shape a thousand colors
each color would have the clear sweet voice
of fulfilled longing.

Because this is not possible
men go out in October
to sit among wet leaves.
Rotted by alcohol,
woodpeckered by doubt,
gnawed by the insect-jaws of jealousy,
they will choose a sound and living tree
that is wholesome and will serve their purposes.
In July when they chop it down,
each chip will be wet with blood.
They will catch it on poles and in their arms

and carry it while women sing
and set it in the ground.
All will dance around the tree.
Some will tie themselves to it
with ropes pegged to their skin
and it will move to the rhythm of their heartbeat
until the thin skin breaks.

Months later, at the pith of winter
in the dead seething emptiness of Christmas
a man will leave off shrieking at his wife
and slam out into the blizzard,
not caring whether he finds his way,
not caring if he is found.

Who Cares

"We have been through the matter of ravens before."
    —John Morgan, Fairbanks, Alaska

Before there was a World, there was Raven.
No sound but the lap of water,
nothing to see but mist.
Of course he made himself a place to stand
and when People came down to the beach
he brought them a little light.
Who cares, he said when they netted
Salmon and cooked him.

That was Food, it was tasty.
Raven cleaned the bones and stood them upright.
Trees. They grew. The People cut them.
Made houses. Boats. Bowls. Bows.
Combs for their women's hair. Masks for their dances.
They carved old Raven potbellied
(*Who cares*, he said)
gross nose, small cranium.

So, he limed them good.
Snow stilled everything.
The People swore: "Though our flint blades snap,
we'll chop through Winter
to get you." *Who cares.*
"We'll take white-hot coal, red ore,
forge tools sharper than stone."
Raven brought back the Sun.
They plucked him anyway.

Down on Two Street,
Raven eyes the dumpster,
sweet as a parakeet, sour as week-old
piss. See him in his thirst.
Oh, foxes bark at midnight, crying
Brother come back to us. He says,
Who cares,
who cares.

Plain Truth (Travis Park Lament)

Plain Truth kissed me natural as rain,
lips soft, mouth calmly open for my tongue.
Men watching TV in that football bar
moaned for yardage. Then she took me home.

There I met her sister Mango Mango
of the Famous Breasts, a well-known
hard case. Breath stopped, knees buckled,
heart raced. My poor joint rose.

Now I've cut my toes off and sleep in Travis Park.
Each night Truth braids
a shirt from her coarse mane
that keeps me, just, from freezing.
This rigmarole has left me far from sane.
Please don't ask me for anything.

Land

My land, you say. You think of yellow wheat,
yellow loess lifting the wheat, a river yellow with silt,
summer and catfish lines and a yellow-haired girl
laughing by the river. But the year is dry,
the unripe corn burns crisp in yellow fields.
Unharnessed horses, listless in bald pastures,
suffer under a bronze-red sun. *Ah my bitter land,*
you say, *Why do you love me so dryly.*

My poor land, you say when you hear the whispers,
votes stolen, women shamed, green fields corrupted,
when you see the dust raised by green-shirted men,
when the balcony above the square clacks with announcements.
My gentle land will be ruined unless I save her.
You imagine grassy hillsides, the green sky after sunset,
a dark-green rye-field with deer grazing,
tart apples and a green-eyed girl dancing under the trees.

Surely my land needs me desperately at last,
you tell yourself. Someone hands you a uniform
and you march with the green men under the yellow dust
banner of drouth and loneliness, to where the air
sings with the razor keen of locusts. You lie down
beneath the dust and grass, and the river goes on running,
the girl dancing, the deer grazing, the land dreaming
black black black black black, all this time.

The Torpedo Angel

Before we killed him
no sky with stars
only the glass floats

of the fishermen.
White in his skin of hooks
he swam between us

and Heaven,
the shining knife of the Law.
His knowledge

rained with the plankton
hissed in the wash of sand
pounded in rocked bells

till we were mad.
What to do? We invented
love, showed him us locked in it,

a sweet and stinking bait.
Our scent spread.
He bit.

Came down as a frail boy
pearl-haired and shell-winged
eyes blue as sea caves

eel between the legs.
Moved between hers. I
slipped behind him,

gripped sun and moon,
slashed quick
with the ragged stone.

Light thickened and was blood.
That sea-age ended
though I carry pain like salt

water in this withered hand
and her sour lips
hide a wet longing—

We breathe clear and dry,
know beauty, are dying
and free. Over his cold eye

we dragged a curtain,
that bright reef
he'd called the Accursed Garden.

They

will go on a long time
after us
with their dogs
mules and tents

avoiding the burned places
the rings the radioactive
cities

They will name us
people of the printed word

Some who set themselves
to learn our languages
will marvel at the subtlety of our thought
and our ignorance of weather

Sun-baked adobe
wall of fitted stone
coyote
lizard
huisache
sage

on toward a mirage
into nowhere
(scrap of a poem
used to line an owl's burrow)

Agave's Waltz
(tune similar to "The Log Driver's Waltz")

Agave pokes spines at the eyes of her friends.
Year by year she grows fatter and meaner.
When the dog who first peed on her lies down with ants,
her *panocha* fills tight with sweet nectar.
She ups a tall pole like the Green Giant's hoe,
howls her *grito* of bats and pale flowers,
decays and dries out to a brittle rosette
and dies to make room for her daughters.

> *You can build a cheap prison to capture the poor,*
> *you can wall off your land and your riches,*
> *but the West Texas moon is a peyote moon*
> *and its light shines on robbers and witches.*

Oh the blood in this ground is not red, white, or brown,
it is black as the stares of Comanches,
and you don't own the vultures that circle your towns
or the sun that pours down on your ranches.
'Gave's older than you, she is older than Time,
she'll be here when your fields are forsaken,
she'll be tossing her hair when your roads lead nowhere
and your cities lie barren and broken.

> *You can build a cheap prison to capture the poor,*
> *you can wall off your land and your riches,*
> *but the West Texas moon is a peyote moon*
> *and its light shines on robbers and witches.*

So breathe in her wild scent as you drink your *mezcal*
or sip your ice-cold margaritas,

or kick back in your chair by the side of the pool
and smile up at the cute *señoritas.*
For the God you profess is impotent at best,
calaveras gaze back from your mirror.
While you were relaxing and taking your rest,
the border just moved ten steps nearer.

> *You can build a cheap prison to capture the poor,*
> *you can wall off your land and your riches,*
> *but the West Texas moon is a peyote moon*
> *and its light shines on robbers and witches.*

Interview

How did you come here?
I swam the river.
Whose is your uniform?
The country of ashes.
What are your colors?
Rags. Bandages.
How many with you?
My son was drowned.

What have you seen?
The air on fire.
What have you heard?
Boots. Screaming.
By day or by night?
By smoke and shadow.
Where is The Enemy?
Underground.

What did you do?
I ran. Survived.
Before the war.
I don't remember.
Did you live in a town?
I lived where a town was.
Describe your neighbors.
Hungry. Cold.

Were your captors kind?
They did more than they had to.

Have you eaten and drunk?
My lips have bled.
Are you ready to die?
I have no questions.
Will you make a statement?
Your weapons are good.

Do you love our country?
My wife waits for me.
Do you hate our pilots?
I have no time.
Do you want to pray?
My hands are shackled.
Any final wishes?
To enter your mind—

To erase the words that inspired an army,
to refute the lie that is written in blood.
To fathom the will that crushed a city
that took so many so long to build.

In Another Country

Who signs with us must lose
an arm or an eye or a baby
or maybe the quiet sense
that the world is home.

Yes, we blow up schools
with joy and abandon,
and, yes, we have drowned our parents
in a dance of blood.

So what if the ghosts of Palmyra
no longer have faces,
if the girls in the towns we've conquered
no longer have souls?

What could it mean to you
if the scrolls of the Timbuktu library
burn to ash, calligraphy legible
in the halls of the dead?

Although we are dead already,
dry sand on a desert wind,
we'll be gods in another time,
in another country.

The Seed: *Danse Macabre*
(to be sung in the voice of crows)

Where ruthlessness is crowned
and no joy can be found,
a seed lies in the ground.

Where justice is ungowned
and mercy's cries are drowned,
a seed lies in the ground.

> *Let life and hope abound*
> *within your walled compound.*
> *Before your gates the starving hound*
> *waits.*

Where gunship rotors pound,
though flames be all around
and razor wire unwound,

below the horror sound
where grave-clods form a mound
a seed lies in the ground.

> *Let peace and love surround*
> *you in your locked compound.*
> *Before your gates the starving hound*
> *waits.*

Granite

No sprinklers whirr to irrigate our crops.
We ditch the flow down every row by hand.
Life is hard in the spirit land.

Some say it's heaven, many think it's hell,
an Earth much like the one we knew before,
with sun and wind and granite. Also hunger.

We rise at dawn and go to bed at dusk.
Hard work wears out our bones and thins our blood.
(The turbines all are jammed in mud,

sealed tight beneath the cracked eroded dams.)
No news, no books, no science. All we know
won't fire a smokestack, might raise harsh tobacco.

Two times each year we meet and pass through you,
your dream of golden thighs and agile cars,
green lawns, green money. This dry world of ours

shares your bright orbit like a stillborn twin.
What you have spent you may not spend again.

Lucille (A Bluesman's Guitar)
(adapted from *La Guitarra* by Federico García Lorca)

Now, the crying
of the guitar.
Barefoot men smash bottles
on the bricks of morning.
The crying
of the guitar.
It's useless.
Don't try to quiet her.
Impossible
to quiet her.
She cries
like monotonous brown water,
like the keening wind
over snow.
Impossible
to quiet her.
She cries for far-off things.
Sands of Africa
that remember white camellias.
Arrow with no target,
twilight with no dawn
and the last bird silent
on its branch.
Lucille!
Grieving child on the block,
pricked gently by your auctioneer's
cold sword.

Milonga de Albornoz
Jorge Luis Borges

Someone has counted the days,
already knows the hour.
Someone for whom there is
no urging and no demur.

Albornoz goes by whistling
a milonga of those times.
Under his hat the morning
is sneaking into his eyes,

the sun the only hero
that day in 1890
on the tough side of Retiro.
No one has kept the tally

of his loves or of the nights
of poker games and knives,
the surly dawns, the fights
with cops and relatives

and strangers like yourself.
More than one cock, more than one bully
has promised him the knife
that is waiting so soon, so early

in a Southside alley's mouth.
Not a single knife, but three.
Yes, he defends himself,
but they're on him like a sky-

full of talons on a rat,
breaking and entering.
Is it that he won't admit it,
or does he die without much caring?

Maybe he'd like to know
he still slouches through history
in this milonga. The tempo
is: two, three: nothing, memory.

Clouds

My grandmother believed
that angels looked down from the clouds.
Anna lived until '64, long enough
to learn that men had flown above the clouds,
above the Earth and, looking down,
had seen no angels.
That year she turned 90.

Once we needed God
to know and forgive our thoughts,
to chart our futures, bring us sun,
or wind, or hail. We prayed to catch the deer,
foil our enemy, grow our food. We prayed
to regain lost love or avoid death
or to take one last longing glance
at the Sears catalog. Now we pray
to remember the God-damned password.

Ah, those online videos
of mating slugs! How I regret studying them.
Steve Badrich, friend, listen to me,
when we are old, when we've forgotten all our passwords,
where is our Cloud,
what Cloud can we believe in?

Able Blues

(with a nod to *They Raided the Joint* by Roy Eldridge and
Hot Lips Page, as performed by Little Joe and the Ramrods
at the Ainsworth City Auditorium, circa 1962)

Because I am
no longer able
I've lost my place
at the head of the table.
> *They dug a six-foot hole and lowered everybody down but me.*
> *They dug a six-foot hole, I was as wobbly as a man could be.*

The names I learned
when I was a boy
are weeds whose roots
I cannot destroy.
> *They dug a six-foot hole and lowered everybody down but me.*
> *They dug a six-foot hole, I was as guilty as a man could be.*

Old people I shamed
are dead and gone.
The remorse I carry
lingers on.
> *They dug a six-foot hole and lowered everybody down but me.*
> *They dug a six-foot hole, I was as lonely as a man could be.*

If words are all
the good I can do,
may they not be for nothing
and no harm fall on you.
> *They dug a six-foot hole and lowered everybody down but me.*
> *They dug a six-foot hole, I was as empty as a man could be.*
> *They dug a six-foot hole, I was a-shakin' like a leaf on a tree.*

Every Season is Hunting Season in Nebraska

September's coming. Skies are clear.
They're painting bleachers for the fair.
The locusts cry another year.

Last night, the Perseids. Now, two deer.
Their startled hooftaps dot the air.
It hasn't rained since you were here.

Our Goldie's losing ground. Her rear
end wobbles when she tries the stair.
The locusts cry another year.

Today I drove to town. No beer,
no friends, no reason. Not much there.
It hasn't rained since you were here.

Our huckster-in-chief peddles fear
and fear sells guns. It's me they scare.
The locusts cry another year.

The locusts cry another year.
I drove to town. Guns everywhere.
Sharp hoofbeats drum the rural air.
It hasn't rained since you were here.

News

Last night's rain has cleared the page
so the only marks I see
are the incised double apostrophes
of the deer,

my bootsoles' bland impressions
from yesterday erased
though a fresh thought seems to follow me
as I go.

Our dogs sniff out old stories
in burrows beside the road
but so far the residents' news
is unrecorded.

While presidents rant like weasels
dry sunflowers scan the gravel,
their unshaved faces lowered
as if they were wise.

Cathedral

Though I have done evil
both by neglect and by intent
I have seen the tiny hoofprints
of the doe's new child
coins not bigger than a penny
divided

Also I have heard
blackbirds in their millions
overflood a grove of naked treetops
with shrill debate

The river's quiet swirl
negates an entire year
of dismal thinking
and the cranes' high trill is a call
to a better life

With these admonishments
and love's warm breath beside me
how shall I stand unmoved
on this crusted star bearing beauty
all we have made and not made
out of malice and kindness

Carved stone upon stone thrown skyward
from the cold dark mud

Dog, Moon, Automobile

I wonder what Flaco thinks
about the moon.
He's looking at it now
as how could he not? It's there,
though the outer edge of the sky
is gold. But quickly fading,
fading.

Soon it will be night
and a dog's best time to sniff
and discover things, and roll in fragrant grass.
But for now,
a-drowse in the lap of love,
he rests his head on my wife's arm,
looking at the moon.

And if he thinks of anything
it is probably the French cheese
I have wrapped and double-wrapped
inside my suitcase.

After the Dinner Party
(for Janice)

Since dusk they have hidden from us,
crouching beneath our chairs
like terriers with greedy noses
hoping for cheese-rind treats.

They have listened to our host
who's recovering from breast cancer
tell us news about her friend
who has cancer of the spine.

The wine has disappeared
like the years of the last decade
when we never attended a party
without thinking we were poor.

As we trudge drunkenly home,
the streetlight shines at our backs.
Our shadows grow taller than we are.
They march swiftly ahead of us.

BOB ROSS (Robert E. Ross) is the son of Edwin Forrest Ross, rancher and real estate agent, and Alice Mary Keech Ross, educator and school librarian. He was born in 1944 in Ainsworth, Nebraska. He is the author (with photographer Margaret MacKichan) of *In the Kingdom of Grass*, published in 1992 by the University of Nebraska Press. More recently, he has published *Billy Above the Roofs* and *Karla or The Weight Liftress*, two short novels, with Stephen F. Austin State University Press. *Those We Can No Longer See* is his second volume of poetry, after *Solitary Confinement*, published by Abattoir Editions in 1975.

Ross is married to Janice Miller of San Antonio, Texas. They live part of the year in San Antonio, and part of the year in a rural house north of Ainsworth, with a good view of the Niobrara River.

Printed in the USA
CPSIA information can be obtained
at www.ICGtesting.com
JSHW020050280924
70526JS00006B/26